MESSY LOVING
A CHRISTIAN GIRL'S COMPANION FOR HEALING AFTER A BREAK-UP

IMANI SHOLA

BOOKS

Copyright © 2021 by Imani Shola

Published by Imani Shola Books

www.imanishola.co.uk

Author photo by Jesse Konadu

With thanks to clairewingfield.co.uk for editorial and publishing support.

All rights reserved.

No part of this book may be reproduced in any form or by any electronic or mechanical means, including information storage and retrieval systems, without written permission from the author, except for the use of brief quotations in a book review.

Dedicated to God – my best friend, First Love, and most skilled teacher.

To Mum, who was and has always been by my side through the ups and downs. Thank you for everything. Thank you for being my role model, confidante and counsellor. I love you.

To Pops – the most intelligent, talented man I know. I love you.

To my future husband: I love you. Here's part of the story that led me to you.

To every woman reading this with a heart broken or healing or healed: I pray you find solidarity and strength in these pages. We are incredibly strong, even before we know it. I honour you.

CONTENTS

Introduction: On this Book	vii
Chapter One: On Us	1
Chapter Two: On Mourning	14
Chapter Three: On Healing	34
Chapter Four: On Helping	46
Chapter Five: On the Other Side	50
Conclusion: On Bright New Beginnings (Reflective Questions)	58
Notes	61
Further Reading	63
About the Author	65
Also by Imani Shola	67

INTRODUCTION: ON THIS BOOK

This book is for Christian women who are currently experiencing (or have ever experienced) the challenging, painful and traumatic season that often follows the end of a romantic relationship.

This book is for Christian women whose hearts have been broken. This book is for Christian women weighed down right now by very real and very valid questions about themselves and their perceptions and their God and their ex-partner and what has just happened. Women who find themselves in a world of grief and confusion and maybe even faithlessness. Women who right now are crying, asking, questioning, why-ing, mourning. Fearing for the future. Fearing from their past. All of those things.

My hope for this book is for it to be, while short and sweet, an aid to you during this season as you walk through and emerge from it. A source of comfort, empathy, understanding and light that meets you where you're at and has space for where you're going. But also a future-focused, hope-filled, tried-and-tested, lived-out map for navigating and, crucially, emerging beautifully from this season – which, by the way, you can and will. You *will* emerge, despite what your very loud thoughts might be telling you right now ('I'll never get over him, you don't understand', 'I'll never meet anyone as good as him'; I do understand because I was there, too). This, too, shall pass: it will end – all seasons have an ending just as they do a beginning – and you'll emerge; but I want you to emerge *well*.

This book aims to empathise and comfort and meet you where you are by sharing my story of my break-up with my first boyfriend after nearly two years of courtship and dating. It will be honest, raw, vulnerable and transparent. I will keep things very real with you. Your healing is very important to me, and I know first-hand that healing doesn't come from image and facades, but from true, honest life experience and encouragement from someone who has walked what you may be experiencing right now. The book aims to reassure and console not by dismissing your questions or offering cheap or easy or '*Christianese*' advice ('pray on it', while helpful, is only helpful to an *extent*, sometimes), but by actively listing the lies and the questions I personally faced after my break-up and that may be tormenting you right now. It hopes to offer answers that helped me debunk those lies and silence those barking questions.

It aims to give you a sense of direction and hope at an often stagnant, silent and heavily burdensome time, by sharing the roadmap that God and I carved out to get me over and out of my own version of it, emerging more radiant, happy, full, fulfilled, fruitful and at peace than I had ever been during or even *before* the relationship. I have full faith in you that you can and will get there, too.

INTRODUCTION: ON THIS BOOK

It aims to be very hands-on, practical and honest with you by suggesting real, sometimes hard steps that may need to be taken to catalyse your healing. You may not agree with the steps; it's important to choose what is right for you. But it'll offer them, all tried and tested, nonetheless. It aims to share a true account of my own journey and, crucially, then present the map of the road I took to healing and the key landmarks along the way.

In all, it hopes to simply be with you *in* the mess – to encourage and comfort you – and then be with as you walk *out* of the mess. Loving sometimes is, or gets, messy. Messy Loving.

I am not a psychologist or therapist; but I *am* a wellbeing champion. If you feel that seeking professional therapeutic help is what you need, please do so.

Lastly, this book is based largely on my experience of a break-up that I went through. It's also worth noting that, as a Christian, I write from a Christian perspective. This book is the map I wish I had when I was going through my own post-break-up season. It therefore does not attempt to speak to situations such as cheating, same-sex relationships, or perhaps where a child was involved, because none of this was my situation. However, I hope that by sharing my own unique story, something in it will speak to yours, to you, to your heart, and that you'll feel all my love and empathy even if our stories are different.

With love,

Imani

CHAPTER ONE: ON US

On You

Hey, girl. How are you?

That's where we're starting.

How are you?

My guess, if you're on the tail end of a break-up, is that you're probably not feeling too great. And that is completely natural. You're allowed to feel every emotion you may be feeling right now. Or maybe you're numb, and not feeling a thing. I completely understand. I was in a similar space towards the end of 2019, having ended a relationship that autumn. I was numb for about seven months after that. It took me about seven months to feel angry and let myself 'be' in that anger for a bit.

We're starting right at day one. Our time in this chapter will be spent helping you during those first few days immediately after the break-up. We'll get into the deeper healing further down the line. But for now, my priority is just to be here with you, sit with you, and let you know I understand. If you feel you're past those initial few days that follow a break-up, you may like to skip this chapter.

How are you?

Maybe you are feeling a sense of shock and denial. I remember the morning after I ended my relationship with my ex, I woke up with a sense of overwhelmingly loud and heavy silence. It can be a real shock: yesterday, you were in a relationship; today, you're single. Your norm of a few months or even many years has changed in a breath. This is especially true if you were with the person for a long time.

I am sending you a virtual hug right now. I also want you to know: it *will* get easier. Time has a wonderful way of facilitating healing. And, as Christians, we know that God is our master physician.

The Bible says He is close to the brokenhearted: 'the Lord is close to the brokenhearted and saves those who are crushed in spirit' (Psalm 34:18). I can tell you first-hand that this is true and that I have lived it. But I also know that right now, me telling you it will get easier is not necessarily the most fruitful or even appropriate thing to do.

None of this chapter is about numbing your feelings, or dismissing them. I want you to feel what you're feeling and know that every feeling is *valid*. But in this chapter I do want to share truths to encourage you, as you feel, and also practical tips for those first few days or weeks after the break-up.

I also want you to know that God is with you right now, right in the midst of wherever you are physically, mentally, spiritually and emotionally. He is so close He can hear you breathing and He cares so deeply about you. He does not delight in suffering. While His love means we each have free will, His love also means that when one person chooses to hurt another, or when two imperfect humans come together and things do not work out, He is close to us and right there with us. As Christians we commune with the God who came down and became like us in human form and felt what human pain felt like: 'Jesus wept,' it says in the Bible's shortest verse, John 11:35.

My four encouragements to you

Here are four things I would say to my past self, the *me* in the days after the relationship ended, with all I've learnt, now over a year since. I hope they can offer you some encouragement.

First, allow your emotions to happen. Let them live and exist. Don't try to bottle them all in or deny them; that could make things worse. And if you feel no emotions, that is also okay.

The point is, however you feel from each minute, hour, day or week to the next, allow yourself to feel it. The feeling just wants to come, have its moment and, eventually, it will pass. Allow it to do so. Grief often comes in waves. Just when you're feeling strongest, it can hit again. That's often its nature. That's okay. Be kind to yourself, understand that healing may be a long-term process, and know that the healthiest way to heal is to healthily acknowledge your thoughts and feelings.

I found that the grief for me started out in waves of swinging from sadness to being okay again. In the days just after the break-up, that cycle would take place from hour to hour. Then, as the weeks passed, they happened every few days. And then, with more time, they would last maybe a day every few weeks or so. That's what my mourning looked like; yours may look different. And that is just as okay. There is a *spectrum* of 'normal', and we're all on it, because grief is so unique to us all. I'm sharing all this just to let you know, if you've never experienced grief before, that what you're feeling today is okay and *normal*, and generally will get better with time's healing. It won't feel like this forever.

Second, I would encourage you to journal. Journal how you're feeling. If you ended the relationship, or know why it ended, journal that, too. Write the facts and your feelings. Writing your emotions out will not only help you process your present *feelings*, but the *facts* that you write in your journal now may save you down the line, too. We'll discuss this in more detail later, but writing the reality of the situation for your records can do a world of good later down the line when you're tempted to romanticise everything that happened in your relationship and maybe even to get back into a relationship that potentially wasn't right for you. So write, write, write. What he did, or didn't do, and how it made you feel. What you did, or didn't do. The *reality* of why things had to end. Why you're confused. Why it hurts. Don't hide anything.

"I'm in between tears and calm," I wrote in my journal the day after my break-up in August 2019. I remember sitting up in bed, writing, feeling numb. "And now it's just this weird dream feeling. Where yesterday you were in a relationship, today you're single. Yesterday you had that covering and protection and hope for the future with that person; today you don't."

Journalling will help you process your emotions, and get them out of your – probably somewhat foggy or chaotic or emotionally tired – mind, onto paper. If you're choosing to 'allow' yourself to feel those feelings, it can be extremely helpful and freeing to channel them through journalling. If you're an empath, especially, or were in a toxic and/or abusive relationship, it is especially important to write to your future self exactly why you left the relationship. This truth may very well set you free later from the oh-so-common temptation victims feel to return to their abusers. It's a cycle we see all the time.

We as humans can sometimes have a habit of, as we go through healing, having moments where we romanticise even the most toxic of relationships, and convince ourselves things 'weren't that bad'. This is where your very raw, honest, real journalling from right in the midst of the situation will save you down the line during those 'rose-tinted' moments.

Third, I want you to know that no matter how you are feeling towards Him right now, God loves you so very deeply, He does not delight in suffering, and He holds your heart so delicately and so dearly near to His own. He *cherishes* you. But He could not force your ex to treat you right and in doing so override his free will as a human being. He also could not, as a loving Father, keep you in a relationship that was, or would have ended up being, toxic for you. Your wellbeing is His top priority. God could only protect you in the process and ensure the relationship didn't get *even* deeper.

Fourth and finally, I encourage you to try to gather a support system around you of people you trust and who know you well. You'll need them as you walk through this season. Whether that's your parents, friends, siblings or a family friend – people you trust to listen to you without judgment and with kindness and patience. For me, it was my Mum and then eventually my therapists.

There is no shame in a break-up

I made the mistake of not telling friends, out of shame, what I was going through. I felt a lot of shame after the break-up, especially being a Christian – as though the fact that it hadn't worked out had proven that it was never of God in the first place. Or that God's way didn't work.

I was scared that people who didn't believe in God would laugh at me and jeer, "Ha! Where's your God now?" I'm now in a place where I believe that sometimes, God does allow hard seasons to happen, but it is only ever for our blossoming and so that we will come out of it better off and stronger. I can tell you that from experience. The break-up is one of the best things that could have happened to me; the growth since, and the core-deep conviction I now have about my own values and what matters to me in a partner and future relationship, are second-to-none. Don't let shame stop you from reaching out to those of your friends who you trust to walk with you through this season. They will be invaluable.

Also, if a *wrong* relationship didn't work out, then it *succeeded*. Read that again. If a relationship that was ill-fitting and not God's best for me did not work out and become permanent in my life, what have I lost? In maths, subtracting a minus or negative number gives a plus. 4 - -2 = 6. Subtracting a liability, a drain, a wrong thing, a toxic situation, a problem, an ill-fitting person from your life is as much a positive 'addition' to your life, a positive and *good* thing, as eventually meeting the right person for you will be. Removal of long-term *pain* from a person's body or life is as positive a moment as the moments of active joy and *pleasure*. I hope that makes sense.

I know it may not feel like it right now, but if that relationship was right for you, it would have worked out – and of course, it still might if it still is and, for instance, someone just needs to mature or it's a 'right person; wrong timing' thing. But you must let go and let God because at this stage neither you or I know what God has planned, and healing starts with accepting the reality that the relationship is over. It hurts, but it is the start of your healing, sis.

My only other advice would be to prioritise your self-care. What filled your life and gave you joy before you met your ex-partner? What are your passions? Is it yoga, or maybe listening to music? Is it songwriting, listening to podcasts, or painting? Is it being out in nature, or reading a good book? Whatever it is, get back to that. Often we can feel lost and directionless in these stagnant moments. Remember always that your core is where your passions are. Slowly, surely, find your way back to those. They will guide you back to your individual self, which so often we lose in another person we were in a relationship with, especially if it was a dysfunctional one.

I am sending you a huge, warm hug. Whenever you are ready, and able, let's move into part two of this chapter. I don't want you to rush this moment. Don't skip ahead to the next section of this book until you're ready to. Take as many days, weeks or months as you need. Give yourself time to think and breathe; time to get your support system in place; time to order yourself a notebook to journal in. This book is not going anywhere; it's here for you for your *whole* journey.

When you're ready, we'll move onto the next section of this chapter. In it, I'll tell you a little about my story, and then we'll get into how to navigate mourning (Chapter Two), the healing (Chapter Three) and helping (Chapter Four), and the other side (Chapter Five).

On Me

When my parents separated when I was 6 years old, I had no idea that deep down a fear of relationship breakdown would be planted into my heart. I saw my parents' deep pain, and all that came with it, and I knew that I didn't ever want to go through the pain of a break-up. I felt their hurt.

Due to a number of other deeply difficult and painful circumstances in the years that followed, involving vulnerable family members facing their own personal and mental health struggles, I also learned to love deeply: love that lets someone hurt it, intentionally or not, over and over, and yet still comes back, because it chooses to believe the best and learns to separate a person from their behaviours. I now know that that is unhealthy love, bordering on codependency. But I learnt to love deeply nonetheless, and also learnt extreme loyalty. I became an empath, too: acutely aware of the negative emotions of those around me, and often taking them on myself, or taking it upon myself to make them right.

And so I came into my first relationship – the one this book will refer to – with a lot of baggage without even knowing it; and without ever having *been* in a romantic relationship. I came with deep-rooted fears and subsequent determination to do all I could on my side to be the perfect girlfriend so that the relationship would work out. (I literally read all the books you could think of on the topic!) And I also showed up with a heart full of love without boundaries; loyalty without limits. It may sound good on the surface, but both put me in prime position to be mistreated, whether intentionally or not, by a partner.

This book is not about to be an account of my relationship; that would be very inappropriate. But I do want to share enough for you to know that I have been there and I know what you *may* be feeling right now.

Long story short, the relationship started off rosy and beautiful, honey-sweet, and lasted for just over a year and a half. It ended in the late summer of 2019, just after we'd both graduated. It had broken down for several reasons, some external pressures we were both facing that were out of our control, but also for some internal reasons – matters we realised we didn't agree on, values we held differently, and problematic behaviours in both of us. Neither of us was perfect and we both made our share of mistakes. Long story short, when I left the relationship I knew I needed and wanted therapy for my share of problematic behaviours, so that I could heal and also so that I wouldn't pass them on to my children, and so I spent a large portion of the end of 2019 and then mid-2020 attending sessions with two incredible therapists.

But my healing was a slow burn. I began writing this book over a year on from the break-up and would say I didn't get over the relationship fully until around March 2020, so about seven months after it ended. And even then, every few months – say when my ex popped up or when I was in my feelings – I would be tempted to go back, to try again. But by then – with the beauty of time spent away from the relationship and spent viewing it objectively – both of us knew it wasn't right.

A year on and I can clearly see the year-long arc of my healing, split pretty neatly into 4 three-month quarters and if you imagine a 'V' shape, it followed that trend. I'll lay it out so that you can perhaps use it to locate where you might be in your own journey. The break-up at the end of August was followed by:

1. **Three months of grieving it.** (September, October, November). Grieving looked like numbness, confusion, shame, distress. Lots of tears, anguish. Sadness, definitely. Loss of trust in God, definitely. This may sound dramatic, but remember I (a) had deep-rooted childhood fears around relationship breakdown tied up in this relationship and (b) had deep-rooted faith in God and the relationship having been His will. So my faith and fears were both completely subverted or inverted by this situation. My faith, I thought, had failed – and my fears had come true. That leads to *deep* grieving.
2. **Three months of still fighting for it.** That childhood loyalty to fight to be near what wasn't necessarily good for me; to maintain relationship with something even when it has proven itself toxic for you (December 2019 to February 2020). Grieving looked like desperation, panic, restlessness, fear. Trying to try again – in my own strength.
3. **The low point in March where I hit rock-bottom.** The bottom of the 'V' shape. Grieving looked like feeling the lowest I'd ever felt. Resignation, hopelessness, numbness again. And then…
4. **Three months of rebirth: things changed.** During that low point in March 2020, I re-read my

journal from the time of the break-up and it dispelled the lies that I'd somehow been disloyal by leaving a relationship that wasn't right for me. During these three subsequent months of finally, day by day getting over it, healing felt *good*. It involved more smiles than tears. Healing looked like getting stuck back into my passions and what makes me feel alive: music and helping others. It involved finding new passions that also incorporated self-care: fitness, as I started training for a half-marathon just to prove to myself I could do it. And as I pursued my passions, I rediscovered myself, and as I rediscovered myself, I understood why the relationship would ultimately never have been right for me.

5. **The final three months** were of *sheer* upward re-ascent: healing looked like continually rediscovering myself and, crucially at this point, falling in love with myself again.

I share this timeline so that you, wherever you are at right now in your own unique journey, might have a map of how long it may take to heal fully and what healing might involve. Remember, your journey is unique and it takes time. I remember seeing absolutely no way out in those first three months of grieving. I felt a grey cloud over my head a lot of the time. I hope this list has shown you how a way out always pans out in the end; there *is* light at the end of the tunnel you are in.

It wasn't all pretty

There were times where even my Mum and I fell out, during the initial six months, as my constant swinging back and forth – because of my loyalty to what wasn't good for me – exhausted her and, understandably, bewildered her. We'll hear from Mum in Chapter Four, in her note of encouragement to other mums.

There were times I sat in the office at work with tears behind my eyes. There was a time I cried in front of my manager; faith and fears subverted, you really do *struggle*. There were times where I vowed never to share any more of my dreams with God because what was the point anyway? I had questions: "Does He actually care about our heart's desires? Is there any point in praying if He does what He wants anyway? Do our prayers for protection work if He'll still let us enter a relationship that's not right for us?"

I've now learnt that God never said we wouldn't go through hard trials; we live in a fallen world, and just like ourselves, those around us have free will and are imperfect. Hurt people will inevitably hurt people. But our prayers of protection work such that if that person isn't right for you, and you're following God's guidance and the Holy Spirit's leading, it will not work out. You'll ultimately be protected, therefore, from what wasn't for you. But having gone through it, you'll also have character and *lived experience* (Romans 5:3-4; Job 23:10; James 1:2-4) – both of which will protect you in future situations with other imperfect, free-will-filled people. It's in touching a hot stove we learn not to do it again because it burns us. Pain is necessary for learning the lessons that will protect us later in life. Shielding a child eternally from pain is not always the best way to protect them – many parents will agree, and God certainly knows that. So while He may allow us to be made into better humans through sometimes painful growth, He never gives us more than we can bear (1 Corinthians 10:13), and He works all things for our good – removing that which is not for our good (Romans 8:28).

Essentially, I believe that God always protects us: directly, by keeping us from what isn't right for us in the first place and giving us clear instruction in the Bible and through the Holy Spirit, and indirectly by the situations He allows us to go through which teach us lessons for later. So both God *and* the situations He walks with us through work always and at all times to protect us – for our good.

So we are convinced that every detail of our lives is continually woven together to fit into God's perfect plan of bringing good into our lives, for we are his lovers who have been called to fulfill his designed purpose.
— Romans 8:28 (TPT).

You're covered, baby girl.

CHAPTER TWO: ON MOURNING

My Mourning Journey

In this chapter, I'll lay out the three stages of my mourning – the initial numbness, then the floods of questions, and finally the lies – and how I dealt with each, so that you are equipped with ways to deal with them, too. With each stage, I share my experience and then the lessons I've learnt, which speak directly to that particular experience. Depending on where you're at in your healing process, you may not want to hear much of this right now. That's okay.

If it's still raw and recent, there's not much I can (or would even want to) say that will speed that healing up – and, let's be clear, I'm not here to do that in this book. Healing *requires* time.

My hope is just that when you're further down the line in your healing process, after some necessary time and space have passed since the relationship, or maybe when you're over the relationship entirely, some of the lessons I share in this chapter will resonate with you. When you're more in 'hindsight and healing' mode than 'real-time and raw' mode.

Remember, this book is here for life, not for one single moment on your healing journey.

Stage 1: Numbness

As I mentioned before, the day after the break-up I felt numb. I remember often saying I felt like a rug had been swept out from beneath my feet. Mourning a relationship isn't easy. I went through a period of self-victimisation, too – where I just felt the whole thing was a cruel joke. I'd prayed to God before the relationship that He wouldn't let me go ahead and enter into it unless it had come from Him. I'd not entered the relationship until I believed it had all the signs of being from God, and until I had peace about entering it. From my teen years, and probably because of my childhood-rooted desire to get my romantic relationships right, I'd been reading books on how to identify a godly man, and how to do relationships well, and here had been a man who had seemed to tick all of those boxes. And yet it hadn't worked out. By the time the relationship was over, I felt there had been no use in all that praying before it at all.

There's no real quick fix to numbness. My advice, if you're feeling this, is just to let the emotions – or lack thereof – run their course. I would suggest backing that full acceptance of your valid emotions and mental space with ensuring you have a support system around you. At least one person you can open up to and just cry with, when and if you need to. My primary support system comprised my Mum, who's always been my best friend. I was also able to find two brilliant therapists, whose objective yet supportive advice was so refreshing (even if, at times, my first no-nonsense therapist's was as blunt as – this said plainly with one highly-unimpressed eyebrow raised and with legs crossed in killer heels – 'I think you should block him.') Then, I also had friends around me – but I want to flag that you may feel like you don't want to talk with your friends about what's going on. I sometimes found it hard being that vulnerable. Sometimes your trust is so shattered by the relationship's breakdown that opening up to friends is the last thing you want to do because your ability to trust even them is damaged. You're in a season where what you thought was for you, and your most intimate relationship, has been subverted. It's natural to want to recoil somewhat from other relationships, too.

My one ask, even if you don't want to speak with friends, is to just have a support system of at least two people where you can. One who knows you well – preferably one who knew you well before the break-up and can redirect you to your core self (as, like I say, we can often lose our sense of self in the other in the relationship and need help recovering this after it ends) – and can offer that intimate emotional support and also help you bounce your emotions. And another, maybe not a family member, who can offer objective, tried-and-tested advice, and also be a listening ear who can give you the appropriate dose of 'tough love' that your emotional supporter might not be able to or know how to.

This two-person, 'one personal confidant and one objective one' set-up also helps ease pressure on your personal confidant, who may have all the best intentions and heart to help you, but may themselves feel overwhelmed or at a loss with how *best* to help you, or feel they can't do it as well as they would like to. Remember, they are not responsible for your healing – you are – and they can only help you as best they know how, and sometimes deep healing – we're talking identifying the deep-rooted, psychological fears, patterns and triggers that shape how you are in your romantic relationships – requires professional help. So your therapist will be there to help unravel the deeper-rooted issues, and equip you (and, indirectly, your personal confidant) with tools to help yourself heal. One thing I also learnt is that a qualified therapist can empower you and equip you with the vocabulary – the technical names – of those things, such as 'attachment style', 'codependency', and 'narcissistic abuse', which will not only empower you to best deal with them, but also validate and humanise your innate feelings and responses. Basically, you'll learn that how you're feeling and responding is very much on the spectrum of 'normal'.

Tough love is important at the right stage in the healing process. Because there comes a point where you have to decide – and this takes time, and you'll know when it's arrived – whether you're going to be consumed by the negative emotions indefinitely, or whether you're going to try to take steps towards healing. And crucially, the decision to heal fully from the pain of a break-up is exactly that: a decision you make one day to do so. It's a conscious, determined resolution in your heart and mind that you *will not* stay here forever; that you will not wallow or allow valid grief to slump into inexcusable, narcissistic self-pity (and yes, self-pity is a form of pride – one that idolises *suffering* rather than the typical pride centred around *success*), because your life is worth too much, and you have bigger, brighter things ahead of you, and a legacy to get on with leaving that only *you* can leave on this earth; a gift to give to this world that only *you* (you alone, in the whole of humanity and history) are wired and able to give.

And then, from that decision, you take action. Which may include getting a therapist. Healing doesn't just *happen* to us. Just like an injured athlete must make conscious decisions to expedite their healing and get back on the playing field, emotional healing takes conscientious action, investment, commitment and resolution. And those all begin with a decision, and a vision of life beyond this grief, as hard as it may seem. You are *not* a victim to your break-up.

Tough love moment over.

Stage 2: Questions

It is completely normal to have questions when something as traumatic as a break-up takes place. Maybe you're questioning whether ending things was the right choice. Perhaps the situation has left you questioning whether the person was ever who they had made themselves out to be, or questioning your own ability to judge character. Or perhaps all of this has left you questioning God.

When I started questioning why God had let it all happen, it inevitably led me to have questions about God and His goodness. I'd been raised in church from around age 7, and was a typical 'church girl' in that I had had all of the values and teachings around things such as signs a man is godly, knowing what to look for in a man that would show he is one who'd lead you closer to Christ. But all of that was thrown into question when it seemed my own judgment – despite all that theoretical knowledge I'd acquired over the years – had let me down in practice. I now know that a man may tick all the boxes in all the books you may read on signs he's godly, and those boxes may well be biblically-based – but if his *heart* and *character* aren't right (or right for *you*), then everything else is a facade. I also learnt it's not your responsibility to condemn, criticise or try to change a person when you notice a character flaw in them. It's your responsibility to accept them as they are. 'Accept', however, does not mean 'enable' – enabling their behaviour. Quite the opposite: it means when God is showing you someone's true colours, you stop trying to paint a different picture. It means taking who they are at face value, leaving the responsibility to change their character rightfully in *their* hands, and putting a boundary in place that limits or removes your exposure to their actions.

As a form of self-protection, I stopped sharing my dreams with God when all the questions around His goodness arose in my heart. Because the dream of a successful and loving relationship had always been so deep-rooted in me and in my childhood, this breakdown of a relationship made me recoil and try to snatch my dream back from God's hands. Remember, I was exposed to the very real 'grown-up' pain of relationship breakdown at the age of 6. I'm an only child, so it was pretty concentrated in its impact. And so the fear for me, even at age 22 when the relationship ended, was real.

I later realised – and only healing can do this, which takes time – that sometimes God allows us to walk through things with Him so that we learn the lessons we need, through feeling, to not only protect us in the future from making the same mistakes, but to empower us to help others going through the same thing. I now don't have to sympathise with someone who is going through relationship breakdown. I can *empathise*. I've been there. And as someone who is called to help people discover and achieve God's dream for their romantic relationships, that is a blessing I can only see now in hindsight. Your test becomes your testimony, and this pain will give you permission and credibility to empathise with those going through similar in future.

I asked questions such as, 'when God says He cares for us, what does that even mean?' In the pain, it felt like He cared but would still let bad things happen to us just to teach us a lesson, and that felt *cruel*. Now, I realise He cares and allows difficult situations to grow in us the backbone and tenacity we need to survive in a fallen world where people have just as much free will to love each other as they do to hurt each other. And that that, in itself, is caring. Caring as opposed to being *controlling*. As is being a God who, while all-powerful, allows us the gift of free will, rather than being one who is authoritarian. Shielding us from pain would smother us, dehumanise us (how could we ever empathise with anyone or feel emotion?). Your pain humanises you, friend. A person who feels no emotion and lacks empathy is a psychopath, a sociopath or a narcissist (or all three in one). And, once healed, your experience protects you. As with the analogy earlier, it's only when you hurt yourself by accidentally touching something hot, and feeling that burn, that you quickly learn how to avoid doing so in future.

Stage 3: lies, delusions and romanticising the toxic

I think the most crucial part in the healing process for me was overcoming the lies I was telling myself and also, really, that my ex in his own hurt would sometimes tell me because he believed them too – that leaving him had made me a disloyal girlfriend; that true 'commitment' meant sticking by your partner's side no matter how they treat you. As an only child, whose friends become like family, and who therefore deems loyalty to be as strong as a family bond, plus as someone whose loyalty had been sharpened during family members' struggles with mental health – where it was my nature to commit to being loyal to someone who was hurting me (even if unintentionally) because I loved them, had compassion, knew they weren't their behaviour, and felt I needed to protect them – the accusation of disloyalty cut deeply.

And while these lies, which come from the enemy (not actually from your ex), can be *tormenting*; the romanticised delusions can be *tempting*. Both are powerful things:

Believing the lies led me to romanticise the relationship and downplay what had gone wrong, in a delusional way that wasn't true to what had actually happened. Lies and delusional romanticisation came at me, hand in hand: the lie that I'd been disloyal, the lie that I should have stuck through repeatedly dismissed needs to prove I was 'committed', the lie that a healthy relationship includes putting up with being treated in a way that goes against your core values, the lie that things hadn't been so bad after all, the lie that it had somehow been my fault. This romanticisation and delusion cycle is natural. And it's where your journals, which I mentioned earlier, will save you.

As the person who had to end the relationship – who initiated the phone call to end things – this was a big one for me. Romanticisation makes you belittle and downplay the *bad* – the bad treatment and, crucially, the negative and painful feelings that led you to break up in the first place. You therefore need to remind yourself of reality – of what really happened and of your feelings' validity.

And there's nothing much more powerful to do this than reading your own words from the time of things going south.

Again, I can only speak from my experience. But especially in relationships where there was mistreatment, or where you struggled with honouring your own boundaries and leaving when they were being dishonoured (as in my case), or where there was abuse, it's this romanticisation that can keep us trapped in a cycle of going back to our ex-partner and their toxic behaviours, especially when we have codependent traits, or childhood trauma that made us 'fixers'. So I'm just here to say: the truth will set you free (John 8:32). Your journals, especially from the time of your break-up, are powerful. Your truth, written raw and real and in real-time in your journals both as the break-up approached and took place and when you started healing – those journal entries addressed to your then *future* self, your now *current* self – are pretty hard to argue against. They are evidence of the reality of the situation you left. And reality will trump romanticism any day, just as truth will always dissemble lies. Those raw feelings recorded on paper will thwart the lies swarming around in your mind. You can answer, for instance, a lie tormenting your mind that says 'in leaving him, you were disloyal,' with the truth that, 'Nope; in leaving, I was loyal to myself and to my mental, physical and emotional wellbeing, which come *first*.' And the Bible backs it up. Just take a read through Ephesians 5:25-33. In God's design, a man is meant to love the woman he is with like Christ loves the Church. As soon as he's consistently acting outside of that, and doesn't want to do the work to change, and you've done all you can on your part, I believe you are well within your rights to question whether you want to be *loyal* to a man who's *disloyal* to that God-given commandment.

If he doesn't want to submit to God, why would you want to submit to him? Take it one step further – would *God* command you to submit to him?

Thwarting the Lies

We've seen, then, how lies in our minds can cause us to romanticise a relationship that wasn't right for us. But how can we combat these lies?

Here's my advice, based on what I did.

Write down every lie that's tormenting your mind right now. Write each one exactly how it's playing, like a broken record, in your mind. Every thought that's also tempting you to go back to a dysfunctional relationship – write it out. Write it in the left-hand column of a two-column table. Write them all down, each in their own row. And then – and only once you've written them *all* down – go through them one by one and, in the right-hand column beside each lie, write a scripture, or simple common-sense truth response to thwart that lie.

In what may be one of the most vulnerable things I'll do in this book, here are two personal examples of mine – the lies in my mind and the responses I wrote for each – to get you started. I promised I'd be real in this book. These have been taken straight from my journal entry on 3 March 2020. I hope they empower you to do a similar exercise. Names have been changed out of respect and for privacy. By the way, every biblical affirmation in my 'Truth' responses is true for you, too:

LIE 1: "You idiot. You gave up too soon and have missed God's best for you. Now you'll have to try to settle for second best in someone else – or you might be single forever."

TRUTH: First, I'm not an idiot. I'm God's child with whom He is well pleased (Matthew 3:17). I'm a royal priesthood (1 Peter 2:9). I was approved by Him before I was even created (Jeremiah 1:5; Psalm 139:13-18). I am fearfully and wonderfully made (Psalm 139:14). I am the very apple of God's eye. I'm His first choice, His precious child, and He sent His first love, Jesus, to die for me (Ephesians 1:3-14). That's how much I'm worth. I'm His hands and feet on this earth, sent to fulfil a mighty purpose that will change lives and nations (John 15:16).

Second, I didn't give up. You're mistaken. I still have faith. Breaking up was never, ever giving up. It was *always* choosing faith: that if God wanted to give the relationship back to me, He would. It was choosing to love so deeply that I surrendered what I had been trying to cling to and make work – a relationship that was heading south – back to God (that's deep love – deeper than the love that tries to hold on with a closed hand and 'control' a person into changing). Sometimes, loving someone means letting them go.

Breaking up was an act of faith and love. After fighting for things to work for a whole summer, two months with little to no affection and no sign that that would change (because whenever I tried to raise it there was resistance), I chose to lay it down at God's feet in surrender, because it was beyond me. Our relationship was God's in the first place and we always committed it to Him. So I surrendered it to Him. And

God will never punish me for doing that. Which leads to my third point: when did surrendering something back to God ever lead Him to give us something worse in return? When does God ever give us bad gifts?

I know that "faith shows **the reality of what we hope for; it is the evidence of things we cannot see**." (Hebrews 11:1 NLT). And that "it is impossible to please God without faith. Anyone who wants to come to him must believe that God exists and that **he rewards those who sincerely seek him**." (Hebrews 11:6).

LIE 2: "You've totally missed God's will for your life because of that mistake."

TRUTH: It wasn't a mistake. It was the best thing possible. The fruit of clinging on and fighting was pain and anguish, I know this from my journals at the time. *[See how your journals are evidence against romanticism?]* I was in pain the more I tried to fight for things. Surrendering was an act of love and trust in God's faithfulness, and of peace. Surrendering something back to God, seeking Him, holding it in an open hand, laying it down when it's beyond you, is never a mistake. And God does not condemn me. Ever. There is now no condemnation for me (Romans 8:1). I think He's pretty proud of me for surrendering what I thought was my promise. Just like Abraham. Let's read it again.

"It was by faith that Abraham **offered Isaac as a sacrifice when God was testing him.** Abraham, who had received God's promises, **was ready to sacrifice his only son, Isaac, even though God had told him, "Isaac is the son through whom your descendants**

will be counted." Abraham reasoned that if Isaac died, **God was able to bring him back to life again.** And in a sense, Abraham did receive his son back from the dead."

Hebrews 11:17-19 NLT

I hope these two examples give you an idea of how to thwart the lies that may lead you back to an Egypt situation – of toxicity and something that was never for you – when God is trying to lead you into Canaan. I cannot recommend this exercise enough. Re-reading them now, over a year on since I wrote them, just to add them into this book, my counter-arguments above really have me in awe. They show me I was stronger than I knew even then. And you are, too.

I'll tell you for free that in the days just prior to this journal entry of combatting lies, I reached a point of feeling suicidal, like there was no hope. Anyone who knows me in person knows I take pride in being a joy-giver as far as I can; in being an uplifter, in making people smile through song, music, good listening and good conversation. At least, I try to. This is because usually I can muster that up in and for myself on-demand; I'm a generally joyful person and thankful to God for this. But the lies were truly tormenting to me. Remember, they preyed on deep-rooted childhood fears and trauma that went to my core.

The day before I wrote those affirmations in response to those lies, I had had tears behind my eyes all day at work, and had then spent my commute home looking at the train tracks I stood in front of while waiting for my tube and overground trains. I got in my car at the end of my commute, to drive home from my local station, and literally bawled. Sat in the car and cried out to God. I said with all my might, tormented by the lies, "Lord, *something* has got to give, and it will *not* be me." A few days prior, my manager at the time had comforted me as I cried to her one day, and asked me if I needed to take some days off – she'd also needed counselling after her own divorce, so was able to relate.

My ex's actions weren't always particularly kind after the break-up, probably and understandably because he was going through his own healing and coping mechanisms, just as I was. I don't blame him – none of this is about blame; we're both human. But while we were generally cordial and friendly, this reality did lead to some difficult exchanges as we both went through our own processes.

It may sound dramatic, but emotional and narcissistic abuse such as gaslighting (again, be it intentional or not), can really lead us to those dark, hopeless places. Especially when it's your first relationship and it's playing on that past trauma that you maybe haven't healed from or even become aware of yet.

It was when I re-read my journals and thwarted the lies with biblical truth that the truth literally set me free. I am welling up just writing about it. Please deal head-on with any lies that are tormenting you, and let the truth set you free.

Once I got to the truth, I found *healing*. That was the end of the low point of the 'V' I described in Chapter One, and the subsequent moment where my ascent into new and full healing began.

Forgiveness

As Christians, we know we're called to forgive (Matthew 18:21-22; Matthew 5:23-24; Matthew 6:15). To 'forgive' doesn't mean to 'forget' – just like to 'accept' doesn't necessarily mean to 'enable'. Wisdom comes from God and God can use lived experience to give us wisdom. Proverbs 2:6-8 (CEV) says:

> All wisdom comes from the Lord,
>> and so do common sense
>> and understanding.
>
> God gives helpful advice
>> to everyone who obeys him
>> and protects all of those
>> who live as they should.
>
> God sees that justice is done,
>> and he watches over everyone
>> who is faithful to him.

Note how wisdom, common sense and understanding are split out in verse 6, that first paragraph. Yet all three come from God. To try to 'forget' what you experienced or what you learnt from the experience of the break-up would be to try to dampen or deny the renewed or refined common sense and understanding that that lived experience has brought you. You learnt lessons from the relationship and its breakdown. Those lessons – that wisdom – are a gift. Lived experience shapes common sense and understanding; and both, in turn, provide wisdom for the future. It's a beautiful pattern.

Yet we are called to forgive. And this is the hard part. I once heard it said that not forgiving someone is like sitting at a table with them, drinking a cup of poison, and waiting for them to die. It is much more about you than it is about them.

Forgiveness is a heart-decision. It's humility: an acceptance of your own imperfection and a recognition of that same human imperfection in the other person. It removes bitterness. It sets you free. And crucially, it allows you to trust and love again in future when the right person comes.

You don't have to tell the other person you've forgiven them. You may not even be able to, if you're no longer in contact. It has absolutely nothing to do with them. And it becomes easier when you realise that people rarely do things *to* us – they more often do things *for* themselves and *always* do things in direct accordance with their own internal coping mechanisms and trigger patterns, healthy or not.

Let's debunk two common myths about forgiveness, and then look at how we can practically forgive:

Myths about forgiveness

It's a one-time decision

First thing to say is, sometimes you have to forgive over and over again. That is completely normal. It may be hour to hour at first, day to day as you heal a little more, and then maybe just every so often as you really start to move on. It may be a decision that needs to happen over and over again.

Like I said earlier, I didn't start feeling *angry* about what had happened in my past relationship until about seven months into my healing process. Until then, I'd still been trying to fight for things, just as I had been doing in the relationship. It was only when I reached that low point in March 2020, just before the two truth-affirming journal entries I shared earlier, that I was exhausted and depleted, tired of banging my head against a door God had clearly closed, and that I was able to feel my anger. Ironically, I'd forgiven my ex as soon as I'd broken up with him in August of 2019 – that was what had kept me fighting for things until March 2020 – that willingness to forgive, reconcile, and try again; to fight for things. But then, when I finally felt *anger* in March, I had to forgive him all over again. Forgiveness, I learnt, is somewhat like an onion; it involves layers, and each time you peel back that armour – reveal that exposed flesh, that wound, that hidden, raw layer – it may make you cry anew. But that is *healing*. I promise. It may not look like it, or feel like it, but it is.

It's a sign of weakness or letting him win

Second thing to say is that forgiveness is strength, not weakness. Defaults are there because they're easy. Stick with me on this.

It's always easy to slip into the 'default': the default way of doing things, the default response to being hurt. If you've only just started working out, and one day about a week into your new commitment decide you can't be bothered, it's easy to slip back into old habits – into your default. We all know this.

If you've lived your life speaking English, but move to France determined to learn French, and a waiter comes and asks you something in French you don't understand, and then he asks you in English, it's easy to default back into English.

If you don't want the hassle of personalising and changing the settings on a system or app, 'default' settings are there for your convenience.

And here, the default response to being hurt by someone's actions or by our own choices, is often bitterness. Bitterness and unforgiveness are common default responses to being hurt. Forgiveness, on the other hand, is the response that takes effort and yet reaps the rewards of healing. Bitterness actually keeps you enslaved to the other person's actions and gives them power over you. It sees yourself as victim. Forgiveness accepts the truth which is actually that your happiness is your own responsibility and no-one can take it from you unless you allow them to. Let's be clear, here, that as Dr Henry Cloud and Dr John Townsend write in their excellent book on the subject, *Boundaries*, we are each responsible **for** ourselves and **to** each other: so while your happiness is your own responsibility, this does not admonish your partner of their responsibility to meet certain needs, as implicated and made necessary by title of 'romantic partner' (e.g. affection, kindness, quality time, etc). With every title comes responsibilities that must be honoured and stewarded well.[1]

So while your partner is responsible to you while they are your partner, they are not responsible for your happiness. You are. Easiest way to allow someone to steal your happiness? Let your emotional state (in this case, bitterness) be shaped by their actions.

How to forgive

So forgiveness is key to healing. And while it may look different for each of us, here is a template of what works for me. It looks like this:

1. Acknowledge: acknowledge the pain. Know, write, journal the way this person hurt you.
2. Lessons: crucially, write what you've learnt from all of this. Objectively, as if writing a guidebook to your future self. Ask yourself, 'what is God teaching me? What would I do differently next time? What have I learnt is important to me in a partner or relationship? What new boundaries will I put in place next time?' This step is beautiful: it's where we see that Proverbs 2:6-8 passage we looked at earlier, in action. It is where past pain translates to lived experience, which then turns into wisdom for future living. This is *growth* and *healing*.
3. Free: set that person free. Set your boundaries based on their behaviour, and release them into that boundaried space. If you still have love for him, feel that love, and then imagine yourself putting it all in a box, and sending it to him. You could write him a letter about what he taught you – again, don't let bitterness fuel it – and then, without him ever seeing that letter, bin it as a sign that you're moving on. All I ask – all God asks, really – is that you don't hold his humanness against him.
4. Repeat steps 1—3 as necessary.

We've covered a lot in this chapter on the subject of mourning. In all things, remember that true, authentic healing can look like mourning. But whether it happens through journalling the lessons you've learned or choosing to forgive when everything in you wants to cling to bitterness, it is always a conscious process and it always ultimately leads to release and freedom. Ultimately, mourning and forgiveness are not easy, but both are necessary prerequisites for true healing.

CHAPTER THREE: ON HEALING

So far in this book, we've walked through those initial difficult days after the break-up, and looked at what mourning might involve; the gritty realities of pain and forgiveness. In this chapter, our focus shifts from pain to healing as we focus on the up-side of the healing process: on the ascent out of those lowest points, and on the upward trajectory towards your brighter new beginnings. I want to use this chapter to equip you with some of the key practical tools that helped me heal from the pain of the break-up. All of these are things that worked wonders for me and which I hope might provide options for you to explore towards your own healing.

I've split the tools into two categories: the 'staples' and the 'catalysts'.

A 'staple' was a tool for healing that was maybe more momentous and more impactful on an internal level. Staples were about ensuring the healing was *deep* and thorough. Think of them as drilling downwards. They were the heavy-weight things that changed my mindset and mentality from the inside out.

The 'catalysts', meanwhile, were more surface-level, practical tools and actions that were all about forward movement. They ensured I was *moving forward* out of that season; progressing towards total healing. They were about propulsion, direction and freedom. Think of them as pushing forwards.

The 'staples' ensured the healing was deep, holistic and thorough. The 'catalysts' ensured the healing only took as long as it absolutely *needed* to.

The Staples

My three key staples were therapy, getting over the idea of 'closure', a term we hear often, and spending time meditating on God's Word. They re-shaped the way I think, made me self-aware, and empowered me to heal fully. In Romans 12:2, we are told in the Bible that renewal of the mind – our thoughts, thought patterns and mindsets – can lead to total transformation. I definitely experienced that with these staples. This stuff works.

Therapy

Therapy was brilliant. I call it a 'staple' because it went deep: it exposed and uprooted some deep-rooted childhood fears and showed me my own negative behavioural and thought patterns up close so I could undo them. It takes two people to make a relationship toxic – actively enabling toxic behaviour is just as problematic as actively displaying it – and therapy helped me define my boundaries for future relationships. I had two therapists over the course of the year following the break-up; the first was a no-nonsense, tough-love, excellent therapist called Konstantina. She was brilliant: she wore high heels, bold lipstick and said it like it was. She taught me much about 'attachment styles' (which I highly recommend you look into to understand your own) and childhood fears. Through my sessions with her, I came to understand how I'd lost myself in the relationship and why I'd stayed so long even though it was clearly toxic. My second therapist, Nadine, a warm and gentle but still tough-loving family friend, taught me about the importance of setting and asserting my boundaries, of being assertive, and of visualising my relationships (not just romantic ones) in outer or inner circles. She also taught me about important terms such as 'narcissism' and 'codependency' – again, two terms I highly suggest you look into if you relate to any of my personal relationship story.

Both of these qualified therapists thoroughly helped validate my emotions and feelings. Therapy is one thing I'll always be glad I invested in and I now believe everyone should consider having a personal therapist as readily as they do a personal doctor or GP. Mental and emotional wellbeing are as important as physical wellbeing. I also strongly believe that it's important that I do the work so that my children don't have to, or at least not as much. So that I don't take subconscious negative thought patterns into parenthood and leave my children needing to heal from what I couldn't be bothered to (given I had the means to).

There can be some taboo around therapy, but I cannot recommend it highly enough. I would encourage you to find a good therapist who you gel with. It may take a few tries to find the right fit, but it can be so beneficial and enlightening to have an expert – who's on your side and wants what's best for you – help you to understand your own mind and triggers so you can manage them well in future, and also understand your partner's, family members', friends', and children's.

The myth of closure

Can you ever really get closure from someone else, or is that something only you are empowered to give yourself? It's a question many of us ask.

One thing that I think was a blessing in my situation was that my ex was usually good at being open to talking things through and listening to my questions. Along with our Christian values of forgiveness and practising the Fruit of the Spirit, it is part of why everything was able to end cordially and with no hard feelings, apart from of course the natural pain of a break-up.

Because I am a ruminator and am quite reflective, and process through talking (or writing), that openness was one of the things I was thankful for in our situation. I don't therefore judge anyone who believes closure may come to them externally, through speaking with their ex. But it is important for me to stress that talking things through with my ex did not give me closure – at any point. We talked for months about things; yet no closure. Talking to him only helped me ascertain where he was at, and helped us both make decisions accordingly.

On the contrary, I gave *myself* closure when I decided to stop pining for something that wasn't right for me.

I'd encourage you to really think about what the term 'closure' means to you: whether it's something that you need someone else to give you, or a decision you're empowered to make and live out for and by yourself. I believe it's the latter.

I know the period after a break-up leads to lots of questions, and especially lots of 'why's. Yet my cousin, a psychologist, once said something so profound to me. She said that knowing the 'why' doesn't actually make anything better. If a close family member dies, knowing the 'why' of a situation doesn't ease the pain in any way. Will knowing your ex's 'why's help you heal, or create more 'why' questions in your own mind?

My cousin's point made me realise that actually, I could let go of needing to know any 'why's. And just free myself to move forward. And that is when freedom came.

The Word of God

God's Word, my third and final 'staple', is so good. It's rich and pure and life-giving. I would say that during my healing process, I really learnt its power.

I would encourage you to spend time meditating on the Word during this season of healing. I believe that one of the things that makes the Word so dynamic is that it has different resonances in different seasons. And I believe there's so much comfort the Holy Spirit, our Comforter, wants to bring us in seasons of mourning and grieving, which often we can access through reading the Word.

I remember clearly around seven months after the break-up (so at my lowest point in my healing process), reading Ecclesiastes

3:1-15 and Psalm 37:23, which I'd read countless times before. But this time, these verses spoke to me in a different way. God was clearly saying to me, "It's time to stop crying." Here's what I wrote in my journal on 8 March 2020, for an example of how I process and analyse the Word and try to apply it to my life.

I've made some notes as I read, and put number markers in brackets (e.g. '(7)') in-line and beside points I've then analysed in a separate list, below:

8 March 2020

Psalm 37:23 says: 'The Lord directs the steps of the godly. He delights in **every detail** of their lives.'

This tells me that God is directing my steps. And that He cares deeply and fully about every detail of every area of my life, especially my deepest dreams. I read this earlier this week and it was confirmed yesterday in a preach I watched, in which the speaker said that God cares about not just my spiritual growth, but EVERY area, including my relationships and my healthy desire to have a life-long, love and warmth and affection filled, successful relationship.

Ecclesiastes 3 (from the Amplified Bible) reads:

'There is a season (a time appointed) for everything and a time for every delight and event or purpose under heaven.' *(1)*

'A time to plant and a time to uproot what is planted.' – This speaks to it being time to uproot childhood trauma patterns.

'A time to weep and a time to laugh;' – This tells me it is okay to have had a mourning season over the relationship.

'A time to mourn and a time to dance.'

'A time to search and a time to give up as lost;' – This confirms it is now time to stop trying, and stop praying about it.

'A time to keep and a time to throw away.' – It is time to throw away the dysfunction. In the relationship, and in my childhood.

'A time to tear apart and a time to sew together;' – Confirms it was time to tear apart that romantic bond. There will be a time to sew together with my future, God-ordained partner.

'A time to keep silent and a time to speak.' – It is time for us to stop speaking with each other, and to allow each other our healing.

'[...] He has made everything beautiful and appropriate *(2)* in its time. He has also planted eternity, a sense of divine purpose, in the human heart — a mysterious longing which nothing under the sun can satisfy except God – yet man cannot find out (comprehend, grasp) what God has done (His overall plan) from the beginning to the end *(3)*.

I know that there is nothing better for them than to rejoice and to do good as long as they live; and also that every man should eat and drink and see and enjoy the good of all his labor *(4)* – it is the gift of God. I know that whatever God does, it endures forever; nothing can be added to it nor can anything be taken from it *(5)*, for God does it so that men will fear and worship Him [with awe-filled reverence, knowing that He is God] *(6)*. That which is has already been, and that which will be has already been *(7)*, for God seeks what has passed by [so that history repeats itself].'

My 7 personal take-aways from this passage:

(1) 'There is a season (a time appointed) for everything and a time for every delight and event or purpose under heaven'. This means that in the book of my life, there is an appointed time and chapter for the man God has for me to enter into my life. It will happen when it is right. Knowing that, it is time to do the work and get ready which looks like: overcoming my idolisation of relationships and uprooting *(v2)* the weeds of childhood trauma.

(2) 'beautiful and appropriate'. Now is not the right time for a relationship. Right now a relationship is not 'appropriate'. There are things to be worked on that my readiness for the appropriate time and season is dependent on. Things that, if not worked on, would wreck my marriage, and a successful marriage is my dream.

(3) 'man cannot find out (comprehend, grasp) what God has done (His overall plan) from the beginning to the end'. This tells me that the relationship was just one chapter in my story and God knows my end from my beginning and all of the chapters to come.

(4) 'rejoice and to do good as long as they live; and also that every man should eat and drink and see and enjoy the good of all his labor'. It is time to get stuck into serving and enjoying my singleness, rejoicing and doing good and eating and drinking and seeing and enjoying the good of my work. It is all a gift from God.

(5) 'whatever God does, it endures forever; nothing can be added to it nor can anything be taken from it'. During this season of intentionally waiting for the right person, I can know and trust that what God will bring together cannot be broken. My healthy, God-ordained relationship will not be broken.

(6) 'God does it so that men will fear and worship Him [with awe-filled reverence, knowing that He is God]'. Everything is done for His glory.

(7) 'That which is has already been, and that which will be has already been'. This tells me that the man God has **predestined** me to be with was chosen for me from the beginning of time. And faith is the assurance that what will be has already been settled and secured and is mine, and I will be able to possess it at the 'appointed time' (verse 1) and the 'beautiful and appropriate' time.

I also suspected, as I meditated on more and more passages as above, that I'd maybe idolised the idea of marriage – possibly because it felt like such an impossible dream for me given my childhood. Sometimes, when there's been family breakdown from young, it can feel like a successful relationship in your *own* life is beyond you – like your fate is set towards failed relationships when that's all you've seen as a child. I realised that, in a weirdly skewed way, I had idolised marriage. I simultaneously wanted to be married one day and get that area right; and yet was also afraid that it wouldn't last.

Are you idolising marriage?

I read a number of great articles and watched some YouTube videos on the topic of knowing if you've idolised marriage, which really helped me discover more on this. I'd encourage you to consider whether you're idolising a relationship right now. There are plenty of great resources out there that can help you with determining this. A channel whose videos I watched often was one called 'ApplyGod'sWord' on YouTube. Generally, though, idolisation looks like the following: a dream, vision or goal that is not surrendered to God. If it's taking over your life, thoughts, and mental space, it may be worth asking yourself frankly whether it's become an idol, regardless of whether or not it's a godly desire at its core (e.g. the desire to one day be married).

The Catalysts

And so the key 'staples' – tools that helped me to do the deep work of healing – were those three: therapy, understanding closure and giving it to myself, and reading and meditating on the Bible.

Meanwhile, my key 'catalysts' that propelled me forward were all about channeling and guarding my energy, and rediscovering and investing in myself. They can be summed up in a short list:

1. **Boundaries on social media**. I found that when the break-up was still very raw, I would see my ex's posts directly, or indirectly, re-shared by our mutual friends, and feel triggered all over again. So around

March 2020, I made the decision to take a break from following him and our mutual friends to really cut down on those triggers. It helped so much! The biggest enemy to this is the belief that you're completely unaffected by triggers on social media such as images relating to your ex. But I realised after a while that I was kidding myself, and needed a break. This was one of the best decisions I made and provided the clarity of mind to move forward, rather than yo-yoing between clarity of mind for a moment, and then being in a state as soon as there was an image of him on my feed.

2. **Tuning back into my gifts and identifying my calling**. Rediscovering my gifts was a huge catalyst towards healing for me. Often, as covered in earlier chapters, we can lose ourselves in a relationship. Then, if that relationship doesn't work out, we're stuck trying to remember or rediscover who we are. This is why I believe it's important to have interests and hobbies outside of your relationship, and ideally ones that start before your relationship. Getting back into singing and writing was for me extremely healing, and also helped me rediscover my value.

3. **Taking up a new hobby (running)**. I took up running in January (2020) to start taking ownership of my fitness. It was one of the best things I could have done. I would encourage you to consider taking up a new hobby – maybe it's a sport, maybe it's working out, maybe joining a choir, learning a new language, or learning an instrument – as that can be brilliant motivation to move forward and it's always good to invest in yourself and pursue new interests. We know

that Jesus came that we would have life 'to the full' (John 10:10). What does 'life to the full' look like for you in this season of self-discovery and rediscovery?

All of these – each of these decisions and actions, each staple and each catalyst – were key in progressing me from 'healing' to 'healed and moved on'. I hope this chapter has given you tools to explore that can help you, too, on your own journey. Please re-read at your leisure, as your healing progresses.

CHAPTER FOUR: ON HELPING

Tunnel End, Into the Light:
A Mum's Perspective on Helping your Daughter Through This Season

Written by my Mum, for parents

"I will show you still a more excellent way." — The Bible, 1 Corinthians 12:31.

Stepping into the light... we are still walking, on a journey, steadily, one foot in front of the other and breathing in – slow, rhythmic, life-giving and full-belly breaths. The tunnel has ended; a new season has begun – it is good to be in the light.

The difference? Now, this time, when I look at my daughter, a woman – blossoming from a recoiled bud into resplendent deeper, more experienced, beauty – smiles back. Eyes – so much happier, twinkling; smile – so much fuller, content; aura – so much bigger, glowing; laughter – so much freer, unhindered. My daughter has done the work, has learnt the love lesson and has moved on. I thank God for His faithfulness through that 'matter-of-the-heart' season. This light is warm.

As a Christian, single-parent mum, I write this chapter in my daughter's book to encourage all parents, but mums especially, to raise our daughters so that they know who they are in Jesus Christ, so that they have their own personal relationship with God, and so that they faithfully trust that He has good plans for them – even when they can't see what those plans are and are tempted to hide their heart from Him. God sees and God knows. Mums, as we raise our girls let's teach them that they are already whole, to believe in themselves and to know-that-they-know-that-they-know that we believe in them, too, no matter what. As a Christian, I know that God's promises are true – if He says it, then it will come to pass. I have seen the faithfulness of God as I've raised my daughter – God hasn't and won't let me down now. He leads me beside still waters (Psalm 23:2) – by His Holy Spirit. This is a truth I've held on to even when I've not been sure of what's going on or how things will pan out. This light is comforting.

I emphasise this because, in matters of the heart when emotions are high, it isn't always easy for our daughters to remember their self-worth, their strength, their gifts or what they bring to the table. Sometimes, in looking outwards towards relationships, daughters can give away much. Unrequited love – spent on a person who doesn't appreciate it or who can't return it – can leave our children open and vulnerable to people with negative voices. These voices often have their own insecurities and areas for development going on. Perhaps through fear, and perhaps unintentionally, these voices can cause our daughters to question the essence of who they are, their generosity, their warmth, their kindness, their love language. However, like mirrors, as mums I believe we should remind our daughters of who they are and of the hole that their uniqueness fills. Dispel the negative with the positive. This light is reflective.

Old things have passed away, and that season is now over for my daughter. But as we walked through it, during the difficult seasons of her growth and healing, I reached up higher, as a mum, in my own walk with God. I prayed a little harder and I spoke His words back to Him, worshipping God in simplicity as I did so. God hears every prayer and loves to be in relationship with us. So – mums, parents – I encourage you to be in relationship with Him. God speaks and He'll work it out – whatever you are going through. We must do our part though in holding our daughters' situations up to God with an open hand, as He is most careful with what we care about. Let's place Him first. Reach for the light.

Seek counsel when you need it – you don't have all of the answers. I'm thankful for my family and friends (whether Christian or of other faiths and beliefs) who shared pearls of wisdom by speaking into my situation so that I could 'safely' talk things through without fear of judgment. Thank you. Harness the light.

And lastly, a final thought. As a mum, I realised a very long time ago that I am not able to protect my daughter from relationship hurts; in fact, to try to do so would be unhealthy for both of us. However, I believe that I have trained Imani up in the way that she should go, as best I know how and as the Bible has taught me to, so that she has what's needed to make God-honouring and life-giving decisions. I thank God for His guidance and for this new season in which He will never leave or forsake mother or daughter, because His plans for us are good and He has a purpose for our lives. His light saves. Thank you, Lord Jesus.

I hope this encourages and empowers other parents walking with their daughters through similar seasons.

CHAPTER FIVE: ON THE OTHER SIDE

So far in this book we've walked through the process from the day after the break-up – and the fog and numbness that can cloud that day. We've also walked through the weeks and months after and looked at tools for healing during that time, to ensure healing is as thorough and as 'efficient', so to speak, as possible.

In this final chapter, I wanted to share a few thoughts on what I've learned looking back. I wanted to share my advice on the 'push and pull' of wanting to try again, or your ex coming back to you wanting to try again. Then, I'll run through where I'm at now (finally free) and what I would say to my past, still-healing self, as someone who is now fully on the other side and has made it through heartbreak. Finally, I'll share some advice on next steps after the healing.

When will I get over him?

I can't say when you'll know you're fully healed. For me, it's been the point of knowing I have no desire to go into anything that isn't right for me – anything that isn't God's best for me. Also, what I find attractive in a person has now been hugely refined and re-hashed. I'm not the same woman I was in my past relationship. Whatever your moment of realising you've healed fully looks like, you'll know that you know that you know when you're there.

Also, don't fret over how long it takes you to heal. Not only is everyone's healing journey and timeline different because no two humans are the same, but the duration of the relationship doesn't necessarily directly and perfectly correlate with the depth of the pain you may be feeling, in my opinion. A one-year abusive (physically or emotionally) relationship could do as much damage as a three-year non-abusive one, in my view. These things can vary so much, and so many factors can be at play, that it's impossible to put a universal timeline to it, and inappropriate to belittle yourself or someone else for how long your or their healing takes.

What I will say, though, is that healing is an intentional process. It takes humility: not only to accept that the relationship is over, but also not to kid yourself that following your ex's social media directly after the break-up is more helpful to your healing than it is a hindrance. The faster you identify and remove the triggers, and dive into your purpose or rediscovering yourself – the faster you reject shame, identify if things like therapy are necessary to help you – the more 'efficient' your healing process will be. It will drag on for no longer than it absolutely *must*.

Push, pull and boundaries

In my experience, an interesting push and pull dynamic can take place after a break-up, where you or your ex-partner may both decide at some point (maybe at the same time as each other) in your missing of one another that you'd like to try again.

My biggest advice would be to pray and ask God for guidance, but also, crucially and on a practical level, to observe if what caused the break-up in the first place has *actually* changed, or been removed. Do not kid yourself in this assessment – it is absolutely key to your own healing and your ex's that you assess whether the factor or obstacle or issue that was strong enough to cause a break-up last time is now a non-issue. For instance, if you were in a long-distance relationship before, the distance was causing insurmountable strain, and now one of you has moved closer to the other, it *may* be worth considering getting back together, if you like.

In my situation, my ex often came back claiming things had changed but soon after would admit himself that they hadn't.

At one point, he got in touch three months in a row, sometimes under the guise of checking up on me, sometimes asking for a call, one time asking for feedback on the relationship. But it became clear, as he told me that he thought I was 'cowardly' to now be speaking with other guys (we weren't together, remember) and that he 'didn't like' feeling like he was only an option now, that it probably wasn't best to proceed.

I, too, would sometimes try to reach out and see if things had changed, but quickly realised each time that the core things that led us to break up were still present. Being real with one another saved us both a lot of heartache. I can imagine that to break up, then get back together, only to break up again is a different level of heartache. And who *really* desires an on-and-off relationship?

But what if I still miss him?

It is absolutely normal to miss your ex-partner if things were generally good or your relationship had started off well. However, this comes back to the point I made in earlier chapters: on romanticisation. As I began my healing journey, I found I only got sad and missed my ex when I dwelt on the 'good' times at the beginning of the relationship. The more I shifted my focus to the realities which led to the break-up, the quicker I was able to move on. My advice would be to ask yourself whether you miss the person, or whether you actually miss:

- being in a relationship – not necessarily with that person (you're feeling lonely, perhaps).
- the good times in the relationship, not the bad times that led to the break-up.

And whether you are ignoring:

- the very real situation(s) that led to the break-up, which were as much a part of your relationship as the good times.
- the very real feelings you felt in the run-up to the break-up.

Let's be clear: missing your ex is a sign of your humanness. You loved him; of course you might miss him. Particularly as you begin your healing journey – in those first few days, weeks and maybe even months following the break-up – there will likely be days you will still miss him; but, in my experience, they will become fewer and farther between as your healing continues over time and you begin to move on. Your ex is probably missing you, too, no matter how much it may look like he has moved on – as I learnt when my ex reached out 13 months after our break-up, asking to have a call or meet for coffee, probably to try again, because he was still finding it hard to move on. We both were still to-ing and fro-ing; feelings are real and I'm not here to play that down.

But eventually, you'll get to a stage where you can say you appreciated the good parts of your time together, and you wish him all the best – you may even still have a different kind of 'love' for him to the one you had before; much more platonic. But once over it, you miss neither him nor the relationship, because it was not right for you or for him. And actually, loving your ex may very well look like making that decision that the relationship is just not right for you – freeing you both up to meet the people who *are* right for you.

If he messages, it's up to you to decide whether you engage with him or not. Once out of the relationship, you don't actually owe him anything, and don't even have to reply. If things are cordial – after a period of healthy space, I would strongly suggest – then you may like to. But if you know you're still raw, or maybe still secretly hoping he'll come back, I'd honestly limit contact. This is solely based on my experience, as with everything in this book. Let yourself heal, hun. There's no rush to be 'cordial' with your ex, even if he is ready to be – or *thinks* he is. Your boundaries in this season matter immensely. Whenever there's a shift in a relationship – romantic or otherwise – it's boundaries that will be what make or break that transition being healthy and legitimate.

If your ex reaches out and asks to try things again saying he's changed, then if you'd like to consider his ask, look at his actions. If you feel safe and his actions show real change, it may be safe to re-assess your boundaries. Do you decide to meet for coffee? If so, even when you meet, look at actions more than words.

If your ex comes back more than once with false promises, and hasn't changed, it may be time for a new boundary. This is where patterns speak louder than actions. As I always say, 'actions speak louder than words, but patterns speak louder than actions.'

Finally free

I am fully healed from, and over, the relationship and break-up, and it is beautiful. I have no desire to be in something that so clearly wasn't right for me. I wouldn't want my ex to be with me either, because I just wasn't right for him. My encouragement to you from this standpoint, now that I'm nearly two years on from my break-up, and with the gift of hindsight? If you know that the relationship ended for good reason, then even if you do miss him at times during your healing, press on into your healing process. Healing is worth the wait and the fight.

I know it hurts. I had days when I missed my ex, thinking he was right for me. I had days when I reached out to him to see if we could work things out. I spent my New Year's Eve of 2019 into 2020, four months after the break-up, having asked him if we could try again and waiting for his reply, which he took a few days to send through – only to change his mind again a few weeks later, then again come back to me again a few months later wanting another shot at things, and *again* a few months after that. So I know the ups and downs, pushes and pulls, and rises and falls are hard. But they are so worth it. Healing is worth it, friend. You *will* get there.

This book came out of a heart to offer advice, comfort and guidance to any woman in a similar situation: in the shadow of a broken relationship. As someone who has gone through and overcome the pain of a break-up first-hand, I know it's a tough season. This season will, however, pass.

Here are some final thoughts I would like to leave you with as you progress through your healing.

- It will get better – trust me.
- What do *you* want? What is important to you? How do you deserve to be treated? Keep these – your values and boundaries – in mind at all times and hold fast to them. They will keep you safe and sane.
- Remember, you owe your ex nothing in this time of healing; it's your decision entirely whether to interact or not. Likewise, they don't owe you anything. We are all responsible to each other as Christians, on a basic level – e.g., to show kindness as far as possible. But kindness can look like boundaries. The point is: don't let anyone manipulate you into anything you don't want to do – and, likewise, avoid entitlement and/or manipulation in your conduct towards others.

- Look at his actions more than his words, and his patterns more than his actions.
- Character shines under pressure and during hard times; meanwhile image shatters. If he's authentic, his character will shine.
- Tune in to how you *feel*. This does not mean be a slave to your emotions. It means get out of your head sometimes and tune into how a man's actions are making you feel: in your body, in your gut, in your spirit, in your intuition. Then align that with how you *want* to feel and be treated (your values). Remember: we train people how to treat us. Use that comparison as a gauge as you then consider next steps and decide whether it is time to communicate, re-communicate, implement new boundaries, or walk away from the situation entirely.
- One more time: his actions speak louder than his words, and his patterns speak louder than his actions. This stands even after the break-up, if not more so.

CONCLUSION: ON BRIGHT NEW BEGINNINGS (REFLECTIVE QUESTIONS)

Whew, have we been on a journey?!

Girl, I am proud of you for making it this far. This stuff isn't easy. Messy loving.

We've gone from what might happen a day after the break-up to looking at what it's like to be finally free, maybe months later. If you've read this book all in one go at a particular point on your journey, don't forget you can use it as an aid and reference throughout your healing journey, coming back to it as and when you reach stages of healing that resonate with what I've shared.

And so, with healing pretty much complete, we come to the topic of how we might make the most of the progress and the situation we've overcome.

I would encourage you to reflect on what you've learnt while going through the process of a relationship breaking down, the break-up, and the aftermath of healing and learning from it.

Remember, lived experience is a gift. I would strongly encourage you to make the most of this rich experience by writing down what you've learnt. Just like journalling, it'll protect you in future.

I would encourage you to spend time thinking about the following as you blossom into your full healing.

1. What do I now know that I value in a partner character-wise? (For example: kindness, being decisive, being emotionally stable, being a man of his word, etc.)
2. What do I now know that I value in a relationship structure-wise? (For example: being friends first, weekly date nights, lots of affection etc.).
3. What are my deal-breakers following this situation?
4. Why was I such a brilliant girlfriend? (A chance to celebrate what you did well!)
5. What have I learnt that I need to work on? (A chance to reflect on things you'd do differently next time.)
6. What kind of love do I actually believe I am deserving of? Do I act accordingly, and is there an issue with my beliefs if it's anything less than 'healthy, reciprocal love'?
7. What, for me, is the difference between a red flag, and something that is just a 'normal' relationship 'up and down'?
8. What have I learnt about myself? (For example: I had surprised myself with how strong I was.)
9. What am I thankful for about this whole experience?
10. What practical steps will I take now to ensure my healing is deep and permanent? Will I start going to

therapy? If I've already started, will I continue and commit to it?

I would also strongly encourage you to deal rightly with what I call the nightmares and the dreams; that is, to healthily approach your fears and your dreams. My suggested way would be to:

1. Intentionally take any of the fears, negative beliefs or unresolved trauma from this relationship (or linked to it) to God and really open up to Him about where you're at.
2. Periodically vision-board what your dream, healthy relationship looks like to you, based on everything you've learnt. What your values are; what you look for in a partner now; how you want to feel in that relationship (for example: loved, adored, valued, etc.). Whatever helps you most.

I believe in you. My prayer is that you will heal and heal well. You can do it. Take your time; do not rush it. Be kind to yourself throughout the process and don't beat yourself up if you feel it's taking too long. Get stuck into community – a great church is a good place to start – and select who is in your 'boardroom' – a name I give your inner-circle friendships and relationships – those people who you can open up to as you go through this season. Don't do it alone.

No matter how slowly it is passing, this too shall pass.

NOTES

CHAPTER TWO: ON MOURNING

1. *Boundaries*, Dr Henry Cloud and Dr John Townsend, 1992, Zondervan, Michigan.

FURTHER READING

Boundaries: When to Say Yes, How to Say No, to Take Control of Your Life. Dr Henry Cloud and Dr John Townsend. (2002, Zondervan)

Attached: Are you Anxious, Avoidant or Secure? How the science of adult attachment can help you find – and keep – love. Dr Amir Levine, Rachel Heller. (2019, Bluebird)

*The Subtle Art of Not Giving a F*ck: A Counterintuitive Approach to Living a Good Life*. Mark Manson. (2016, Harper)

ABOUT THE AUTHOR

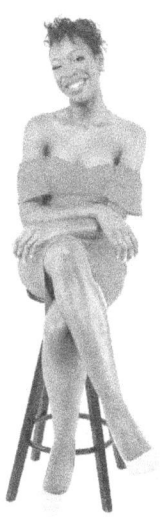

Imani Shola is a Christian author, music artist and creative from London.

A recent Cambridge University graduate, she is also a former Commended Winner of the prestigious Foyle Young Poet of the Year Award, the world's largest award for young poets, attracting tens of thousands of entries from over 70 countries each year.

Her debut collection of self-care poetry and affirmative notes, *Heart Shards and Lip Balm*, was released in 2017 and has been read by readers from Australia to Canada, Norway to the States, and Singapore to South Africa.

Imani's heart is simply to love others and to help them heal, grow and excel. If this book has touched you, please consider spreading the word and leaving a review on Amazon, Goodreads or any other suitable forum.

imanishola.co.uk

 x.com/imanishola
 instagram.com/imanishola

ALSO BY IMANI SHOLA

Heart Shards and Lip Balm: 100 self-care poems and affirmative notes for your journey

Penned to help those suffering from heartbreak, emotional pain and disillusionment, ***Heart Shards and Lip Balm*** is the debut self-care poetry collection of former Commended UK Foyle Young Poet of the Year, Imani Shola.

Andrews McMeel Publishing, publishers of New York Times bestselling self-care collection, ***Milk and Honey* by Rupi Kaur**, describe Imani's poetry as possessing **'a beautiful voice'** and have honoured her collection's outstanding **'concept and heart'**. The collection of 100 self-care poems and affirmative notes-to-reader offers readers what Imani describes as 'love in book form', in radical response to the epidemic of depression amongst the millennial generation to which she belongs, and to recent tragedies tearing across Britain.

Heart Shards and Lip Balm, written by the author at age 20 as she balanced her full-time Cambridge studies with managing her online platforms, offers explorations and reflections on everything from **terrorism**, **the impacts of social media upon millennials**, **sexual abuse**, **mental illness**, depression, and immigration and the experience of the diaspora, to Imani's experiences as a **woman of colour**, femininity, family breakdown, faith, betrayal, romance, heartbreak and disillusionment. It traces the journey from heartbreak to healing by offering readers heartfelt reassurance in proverb-style wisdom poems and affirmative self-care reminders.

"The collection came from a desire to love on my generation," says Imani, "among whom depression and a real lack of **self-care and self-esteem** are rife. I saw it among my peers and it breaks my heart. I wanted to make a radical, positive change – so I wrote a book."

Imani isn't wrong; the book's message of self-care from one millennial to millions across the globe could not come at a better time, since studies show that **the millennial generation is suffering from higher depression rates** than their Generation X counterparts and almost 40 percent of millennials say their stress is increasing. And in the US alone, between 2005 and 2014, the number of depressed teens increased by more than half a million – three-fourths of which were teenage girls, the main audience for the book.

A past winner of the world's **most prestigious award** for poets aged 11—17 writing original works in English, the Foyle Young Poets of the Year Award, Imani is already a bourgeoning force on the British poetry scene. She was named a commended winner at age 14 by **Imtiaz Dharker** and **Glyn Maxwell**. The annual competition, which attracts over 10,000 entries from more than 6,000 poets across

76 countries, is run by The Poetry Society, whose famous National Poetry Competition has kickstarted the careers of the likes of British Poet Laureate, Dame Carol Ann Duffy.

www.ingramcontent.com/pod-product-compliance
Lightning Source LLC
Chambersburg PA
CBHW071221070526
44584CB00019B/3106